Let's Find Out Readers

Look Up In the Sky

By Pamela Chanko

SCHOLASTIC

Look Up In the Sky

By Pamela Chanko

No part of this publication can be reproduced in whole or in part, or stored in a retrieval system, or transmitted in any form or by any means, electronic, mechanical, photocopying, recording, or otherwise, without written permission of the publisher. For permission, write to Scholastic Inc., 557 Broadway, New York, NY 10012.

ISBN: 978-1-338-88850-8

Editor: Liza Charlesworth
Art Director: Tannaz Fassihi; Designer: Tanya Chernyak
Photos ©: Vicki Jauron, Babylon and Beyond Photography/Getty Images.
All other photos © Shutterstock.com.

Copyright © Scholastic Inc. All rights reserved. Published by Scholastic Inc.

1 2 3 4 5 6 7 8 9 10 68 31 30 29 28 27 26 25 24 23

Printed in Jiaxing, China. First printing, January 2023.

SCHOLASTIC INC.

There is a cloud.

There is a plane.

There is a bird.

There is a helicopter.

There is a balloon.

There is a rainbow.

There is a kite!

Let's Find Out Readers

ISBN: 978-1-338-88850-

SCHOLASTIC

9 781338 888508

Let's Find Out Readers

In My Classroom

By Pamela Chanko

In My Classroom

By Pamela Chanko

No part of this publication can be reproduced in whole or in part, or stored in a retrieval system, or transmitted in any form or by any means, electronic, mechanical, photocopying, recording, or otherwise, without written permission of the publisher. For permission, write to Scholastic Inc., 557 Broadway, New York, NY 10012.

ISBN: 978-1-338-88851-5

Editor: Liza Charlesworth
Art Director: Tannaz Fassihi; Designer: Tanya Chernyak
Photos ©: cover: Karen Roach/Shutterstock.com; 2: nico_blue/Getty Images;
3: ideabug/Getty Images; 4: Kevin Giszewski/Dreamstime; 5: Llewellyn/Alamy Stock Photo;
6: photonic 1/Alamy Stock Photo; 7: m.schuppich/Alamy Stock Photo; 8: FatCamera/Getty Images.

Copyright © Scholastic Inc. All rights reserved. Published by Scholastic Inc.

1 2 3 4 5 6 7 8 9 10   68   31 30 29 28 27 26 25 24 23

Printed in Jiaxing, China. First printing, January 2023.

SCHOLASTIC INC.

We have pencils.

We have paper.

We have crayons.

We have paints.

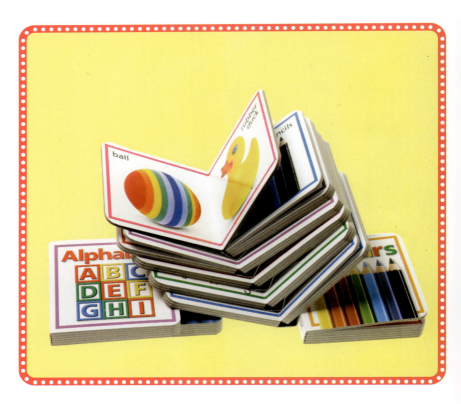

We have books.

We have blocks.

We have kids!

Let's Find Out® Readers

ISBN: 978-1-338-88851

SCHOLASTIC

Let's Find Out Readers

I See Numbers

By Pamela Chanko

SCHOLASTIC

I See Numbers

By Pamela Chanko

No part of this publication can be reproduced in whole or in part, or stored in a retrieval system, or transmitted in any form or by any means, electronic, mechanical, photocopying, recording, or otherwise, without written permission of the publisher. For permission, write to Scholastic Inc., 557 Broadway, New York, NY 10012.

ISBN: 978-1-338-88852-2

Editor: Liza Charlesworth
Art Director: Tannaz Fassihi; Designer: Tanya Chernyak
Photos ©: 4: clu/Getty Images; 7: Mouse in the House/Alamy Stock Photo;
8: dubassy/Getty Images. All other photos © Shutterstock.com.

Copyright © Scholastic Inc. All rights reserved. Published by Scholastic Inc.

1 2 3 4 5 6 7 8 9 10 68 31 30 29 28 27 26 25 24 23

Printed in Jiaxing, China. First printing, January 2023.

SCHOLASTIC INC.

I see numbers on a train.

I see numbers on a game.

I see numbers on a clock.

I see numbers on a door.

I see numbers on a shirt.

I see numbers on a phone.

I see numbers in my soup!

ISBN: 978-1-338-88852

9 781338 888522

Let's Find Out Readers

Playground Fun

By Janice Behrens

Playground Fun

By Janice Behrens

No part of this publication can be reproduced in whole or in part, or stored in a retrieval system, or transmitted in any form or by any means, electronic, mechanical, photocopying, recording, or otherwise, without written permission of the publisher. For permission, write to Scholastic Inc., 557 Broadway, New York, NY 10012.

ISBN: 978-1-338-88853-9

Editor: Liza Charlesworth
Art Director: Tannaz Fassihi; Designer: Tanya Chernyak
Photos ©: JGI/Daniel Grill/Getty Images; 3: skynesher/Getty Images;
4: gpointstudio/Getty Images; 6: Kontrec/Getty Images; 7: monkeybusinessimages/Getty Images.
All other photos © Shutterstock.com.

Copyright © Scholastic Inc. All rights reserved. Published by Scholastic Inc.

1 2 3 4 5 6 7 8 9 10   68   31 30 29 28 27 26 25 24 23

Printed in Jiaxing, China. First printing, January 2023.

SCHOLASTIC INC.

This is where kids swing.

This is where kids slide.

This is where kids dig.

This is where kids climb.

This is where kids hop.

This is where kids run.

This is where kids smile!

Let's Find Out Readers

ISBN: 978-1-338-88853

Scholastic

9 781338 888539

Let's Find Out Readers

Happy Birthday!

By Janice Behrens

SCHOLASTIC

Happy Birthday!

By Janice Behrens

No part of this publication can be reproduced in whole or in part, or stored in a retrieval system, or transmitted in any form or by any means, electronic, mechanical, photocopying, recording, or otherwise, without written permission of the publisher. For permission, write to Scholastic Inc., 557 Broadway, New York, NY 10012.

ISBN: 978-1-338-88854-6

Editor: Liza Charlesworth
Art Director: Tannaz Fassihi; Designer: Tanya Chernyak
Photos ©: 5: Stefan Stanisavljevic/Getty Images; 6: juliannafunk/Getty Images; 7: DEMIURGE_100/Getty Images; 8: Burke/Triolo Productions/Getty Images. All other photos © Shutterstock.com.

Copyright © Scholastic Inc. All rights reserved. Published by Scholastic Inc.

1 2 3 4 5 6 7 8 9 10   68   31 30 29 28 27 26 25 24 23

Printed in Jiaxing, China. First printing, January 2023.

SCHOLASTIC INC.

Get the birthday hats.

Get the birthday presents.

Get the birthday balloons.

Get the birthday plates.

Get the birthday cake.

Get the birthday candles.

Happy birthday!

Let's Find Out Readers

ISBN: 978-1-338-88854-

SCHOLASTIC

Let's Find Out Readers

We Like to Play

By Pamela Chanko

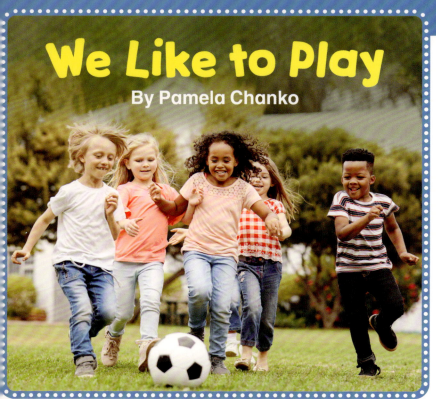

Scholastic

We Like to Play

By Pamela Chanko

No part of this publication can be reproduced in whole or in part, or stored in a retrieval system, or transmitted in any form or by any means, electronic, mechanical, photocopying, recording, or otherwise, without written permission of the publisher. For permission, write to Scholastic Inc., 557 Broadway, New York, NY 10012.

ISBN: 978-1-338-88855-3

Editor: Liza Charlesworth
Art Director: Tannaz Fassihi; Designer: Tanya Chernyak
Photo ©: 3: Bull&;#39;s-Eye Visual Arts/Shutterstock.com. All other photos © Getty Images.

Copyright © Scholastic Inc. All rights reserved. Published by Scholastic Inc.

1 2 3 4 5 6 7 8 9 10   68   31 30 29 28 27 26 25 24 23

Printed in Jiaxing, China. First printing, January 2023.

SCHOLASTIC INC.

I like to play soccer.
I have fun!

I like to play softball.
I have fun!

I like to play basketball.
I have fun!

I like to play tennis.
I have fun!

I like to play football.
I have fun!

I like to play hockey.
I have fun!

We like to play together.
We have fun!

Let's Find Out® Readers

ISBN: 978-1-338-88855-

Let's Find Out Readers

Supermarket Soup

By Pamela Chanko

Supermarket Soup

By Pamela Chanko

No part of this publication can be reproduced in whole or in part, or stored in a retrieval system, or transmitted in any form or by any means, electronic, mechanical, photocopying, recording, or otherwise, without written permission of the publisher. For permission, write to Scholastic Inc., 557 Broadway, New York, NY 10012.

ISBN: 978-1-338-88856-0

Editor: Liza Charlesworth
Art Director: Tannaz Fassihi; Designer: Tanya Chernyak
Photos ©: cover: Africa Studio/Shutterstock.com; 6: mohd kamarul hafiz/Shutterstock.com.
All other photos © Getty Images.

Copyright © Scholastic Inc. All rights reserved. Published by Scholastic Inc.

1 2 3 4 5 6 7 8 9 10   68   31 30 29 28 27 26 25 24 23

Printed in Jiaxing, China. First printing, January 2023.

SCHOLASTIC INC.

I help get the carrots.
Mmm, mmm, carrots!

I help get the celery.
Mmm, mmm, celery!

I help get the tomatoes.
Mmm, mmm, tomatoes!

I help get the potatoes.
Mmm, mmm, potatoes!

I help get the corn.
Mmm, mmm, corn!

I help get the noodles.
Mmm, mmm, noodles!

I help eat the soup.
Mmm, mmm, soup!

Let's Find Out® Readers

ISBN: 978-1-338-88856-

SCHOLASTIC

9 781338 888560

Let's Find Out Readers

We Walk Dogs

By Janice Behrens

Scholastic

We Walk Dogs

By Janice Behrens

No part of this publication can be reproduced in whole or in part, or stored in a retrieval system, or transmitted in any form or by any means, electronic, mechanical, photocopying, recording, or otherwise, without written permission of the publisher. For permission, write to Scholastic Inc., 557 Broadway, New York, NY 10012.

ISBN: 978-1-338-88857-7

Editor: Liza Charlesworth
Art Director: Tannaz Fassihi; Designer: Tanya Chernyak
Photos ©: 5: Roman Samborskyi/Shutterstock.com. All other photos © Getty Images.

Copyright © Scholastic Inc. All rights reserved. Published by Scholastic Inc.
1 2 3 4 5 6 7 8 9 10   68   31 30 29 28 27 26 25 24 23
Printed in Jiaxing, China. First printing, January 2023.

SCHOLASTIC INC.

We walk dogs.

Woof, woof.

We walk big dogs.
Woof, woof.

We walk small dogs.
Woof, woof.

We walk fluffy dogs.
Woof, woof.

We walk puppy dogs.
Woof, woof.

But we do not walk cats.
Meow, meow.

Let's Find Out® Readers

ISBN: 978-1-338-88857-

Let's Find Out Readers

Bubble, Bubble

By Janice Behrens

SCHOLASTIC

Bubble, Bubble

By Janice Behrens

No part of this publication can be reproduced in whole or in part, or stored in a retrieval system, or transmitted in any form or by any means, electronic, mechanical, photocopying, recording, or otherwise, without written permission of the publisher. For permission, write to Scholastic Inc., 557 Broadway, New York, NY 10012.

ISBN: 978-1-338-88858-4

Editor: Liza Charlesworth
Art Director: Tannaz Fassihi; Designer: Tanya Chernyak
Photos ©: 5 Breslavtsev Oleg/Shutterstock.com; 8: stopabox/Shutterstock.com.
All other photos © Getty Images.

Copyright © Scholastic Inc. All rights reserved. Published by Scholastic Inc.

1 2 3 4 5 6 7 8 9 10   68   31 30 29 28 27 26 25 24 23

Printed in Jiaxing, China. First printing, January 2023.

SCHOLASTIC INC.

Bubble, bubble, milk bubbles.
Will they pop?

Bubble, bubble, gum bubbles.
Will they pop?

Bubble, bubble, fish bubbles.
Will they pop?

Bubble, bubble, bath bubbles.
Will they pop?

Bubble, bubble, snail bubbles.
Will they pop?

Bubble, bubble, soap bubbles.
Will they pop?

Yes.
POP!

Let's Find Out
Readers

SCHOLASTIC

ISBN: 978-1-338-88858-4

Let's Find Out Readers

Are We There Yet?

By Janice Behrens

Are We There Yet?

By Janice Behrens

No part of this publication can be reproduced in whole or in part, or stored in a retrieval system, or transmitted in any form or by any means, electronic, mechanical, photocopying, recording, or otherwise, without written permission of the publisher. For permission, write to Scholastic Inc., 557 Broadway, New York, NY 10012.

ISBN: 978-1-338-88859-1

Editor: Liza Charlesworth
Art Director: Tannaz Fassihi; Designer: Tanya Chernyak
Photos ©: 2: Rune Hellestad/Getty Images; 5: Sami Sarkis Travel/Alamy Stock Photo; 6: HBpictures/Adobe Stock; 7: Orbon Alija/Getty Images; 8: FangXiaNuo/Getty Images. All other photos © Shutterstock.com.

Copyright © Scholastic Inc. All rights reserved. Published by Scholastic Inc.
1 2 3 4 5 6 7 8 9 10   68   31 30 29 28 27 26 25 24 23
Printed in Jiaxing, China. First printing, January 2023.

SCHOLASTIC INC.

We read in the car.
Are we there yet?

We sing in the car.
Are we there yet?

We eat in the car.
Are we there yet?

We draw in the car.
Are we there yet?

We laugh in the car.
Are we there yet?

We sleep in the car.
Are we there yet?

Yes!

Let's Find Out® Readers

ISBN: 978-1-338-88859-1

SCHOLASTIC

Let's Find Out Readers

We Help in the Garden

By Janice Behrens

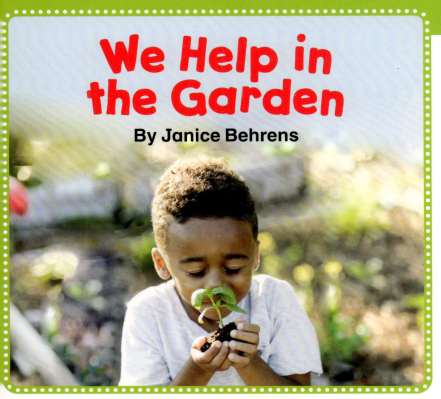

SCHOLASTIC

We Help in the Garden

By Janice Behrens

No part of this publication can be reproduced in whole or in part, or stored in a retrieval system, or transmitted in any form or by any means, electronic, mechanical, photocopying, recording, or otherwise, without written permission of the publisher. For permission, write to Scholastic Inc., 557 Broadway, New York, NY 10012.

ISBN: 978-1-338-88860-7

Editor: Liza Charlesworth
Art Director: Tannaz Fassihi; Designer: Tanya Chernyak
Photos ©: 3: A3pfamily/Shutterstock.com.; 6: kochabamba/Shutterstock.com.
All other photos © Getty Images.

Copyright © Scholastic Inc. All rights reserved. Published by Scholastic Inc.

1 2 3 4 5 6 7 8 9 10   68   31 30 29 28 27 26 25 24 23

Printed in Jiaxing, China. First printing, January 2023.

SCHOLASTIC INC.

I get to dig the dirt.
Is that the best job?

I get to plant the flowers.
Is that the best job?

I get to carry the flowers.
Is that the best job?

I get to water the flowers.
Is that the best job?

I get to paint the fence.
Is that the best job?

I get to pick the carrots.
Is that the best job?

I get to eat the carrots.
Is that the best job?
Yes, it is!

Let's Find Out Readers

ISBN: 978-1-338-88860-7

Let's Find Out Readers

What Has Wheels?

By Pamela Chanko

Scholastic

What Has Wheels?

By Pamela Chanko

No part of this publication can be reproduced in whole or in part, or stored in a retrieval system, or transmitted in any form or by any means, electronic, mechanical, photocopying, recording, or otherwise, without written permission of the publisher. For permission, write to Scholastic Inc., 557 Broadway, New York, NY 10012.

ISBN: 978-1-338-88862-1

Editor: Liza Charlesworth
Art Director: Tannaz Fassihi; Designer: Tanya Chernyak
All photos © Shutterstock.com.

Copyright © Scholastic Inc. All rights reserved. Published by Scholastic Inc.
1 2 3 4 5 6 7 8 9 10   68   31 30 29 28 27 26 25 24 23
Printed in Jiaxing, China. First printing, January 2023.

SCHOLASTIC INC.

What has wheels?
This green car has wheels.

What has wheels?
This yellow bus has wheels.

What has wheels?
This orange bike has wheels.

What has wheels?
This red truck has wheels.

What has wheels?
This blue van has wheels.

What has wheels?
This silver cart has wheels.

Who has wheels?
These cool kids have wheels!
ZOOM, ZOOM!

Let's Find Out® Readers

SCHOLASTIC

ISBN: 978-1-338-88862-1

Let's Find Out Readers

I Want to Be a Firefighter

By Janice Behrens

SCHOLASTIC

I Want to Be a Firefighter

By Janice Behrens

No part of this publication can be reproduced in whole or in part, or stored in a retrieval system, or transmitted in any form or by any means, electronic, mechanical, photocopying, recording, or otherwise, without written permission of the publisher. For permission, write to Scholastic Inc., 557 Broadway, New York, NY 10012.

ISBN: 978-1-338-88863-8

Editor: Liza Charlesworth
Art Director: Tannaz Fassihi; Designer: Tanya Chernyak
Photos ©: cover: kali9/Getty Images; 3: kali9/Getty Images; 5: Mike295855/Getty Images; 6: LightField Studios Inc./Alamy Stock Photo; 7: George Shelley/Getty Images; 8: McIninch/Getty Images. All other photos © Shutterstock.com.

Copyright © Scholastic Inc. All rights reserved. Published by Scholastic Inc.

1 2 3 4 5 6 7 8 9 10   68   31 30 29 28 27 26 25 24 23

Printed in Jiaxing, China. First printing, January 2023.

SCHOLASTIC INC.

I want to drive the firetruck.
Do you?

I want to put on the hat.
Do you?

I want to slide down the pole.
Do you?

I want to climb up the ladder.
Do you?

I want to spray the hose.
Do you?

I want to hug the dog.
Do you?

Let's Find Out Readers

SCHOLASTIC

ISBN: 978-1-338-88863-

Let's Find Out Readers

All Aboard!

By Pamela Chanko

SCHOLASTIC

All Aboard!

By Pamela Chanko

No part of this publication can be reproduced in whole or in part, or stored in a retrieval system, or transmitted in any form or by any means, electronic, mechanical, photocopying, recording, or otherwise, without written permission of the publisher. For permission, write to Scholastic Inc., 557 Broadway, New York, NY 10012.

ISBN: 978-1-338-88864-5

Editor: Liza Charlesworth
Art Director: Tannaz Fassihi; Designer: Tanya Chernyak
Photos ©: 4: Vladimir Fomin/Dreamstime; 6: LIVINUS/Getty Images; 7: Imel9000/Getty Images; 8: Arjo Van Timmeren / EyeEm/Getty Images. All other photos © Shutterstock.com.

Copyright © Scholastic Inc. All rights reserved. Published by Scholastic Inc.

1 2 3 4 5 6 7 8 9 10   68   31 30 29 28 27 26 25 24 23

Printed in Jiaxing, China. First printing, January 2023.

SCHOLASTIC INC.

You can ride on a train.
All aboard!

You can fly on a plane.
All aboard!

You can ride on a bus.
All aboard!

You can sail on a boat.
All aboard!

You can ride on a trolley.
All aboard!

You can float in a balloon.
All aboard!

You can ride on a merry-go-round.
All aboard!

ISBN: 978-1-338-88864-5

Let's Find Out Readers

A Cold, Cold Day
By Pamela Chanko

SCHOLASTIC

A Cold, Cold Day

By Pamela Chanko

No part of this publication can be reproduced in whole or in part, or stored in a retrieval system, or transmitted in any form or by any means, electronic, mechanical, photocopying, recording, or otherwise, without written permission of the publisher. For permission, write to Scholastic Inc., 557 Broadway, New York, NY 10012.

ISBN: 978-1-338-88865-2

Editor: Liza Charlesworth
Art Director: Tannaz Fassihi; Designer: Tanya Chernyak
Photos ©: 6: Chubykin Arkady/Shutterstock.com; 7: gorillaimages/Shutterstock.com; 8: Yuganov Konstantin/Shutterstock.com. All other photos © Getty Images.

Copyright © Scholastic Inc. All rights reserved. Published by Scholastic Inc.

1 2 3 4 5 6 7 8 9 10   68   31 30 29 28 27 26 25 24 23

Printed in Jiaxing, China. First printing, January 2023.

SCHOLASTIC INC.

It is a cold, cold day!
Time to ride on a sled.

It is a cold, cold day!
Time to build a snowman.

It is a cold, cold day!
Time to throw a snowball.

It is a cold, cold day!
Time to ice skate.

It is a cold, cold day!
Time to build a fort.

It is a cold, cold day!
Time to make a snow angel.

It is a cold, cold day!
Time to get warm.

ISBN: 978-1-338-88865-2

What Pet Would You Get?

By Pamela Chanko

Scholastic

What Pet Would You Get?

By Pamela Chanko

No part of this publication can be reproduced in whole or in part, or stored in a retrieval system, or transmitted in any form or by any means, electronic, mechanical, photocopying, recording, or otherwise, without written permission of the publisher. For permission, write to Scholastic Inc., 557 Broadway, New York, NY 10012.

ISBN: 978-1-338-88866-9

Editor: Liza Charlesworth
Art Director: Tannaz Fassihi; Designer: Tanya Chernyak
Photos ©: 3: ultura Creative RF/Alamy Stock Photo; 5: Randy Faris/Getty Images; 8: Cavan Images/Getty Images. All other photos © Shutterstock.com.

Copyright © Scholastic Inc. All rights reserved. Published by Scholastic Inc.
1 2 3 4 5 6 7 8 9 10   68   31 30 29 28 27 26 25 24 23
Printed in Jiaxing, China. First printing, January 2023.

SCHOLASTIC INC.

This dog is friendly.
Would you get this pet?
Maybe!

This cat is sleepy.
Would you get this pet?
Maybe!

This bunny is soft and cuddly.
Would you get this pet?
Maybe!

This fish is orange.
Would you get this pet?
Maybe!

This bird is able to talk.
Would you get this pet?
Maybe!

This turtle is very tiny.
Would you get this pet?
Maybe!

This elephant is HUGE!
Would you get this pet?
Maybe...not!

Let's Find Out Readers

ISBN: 978-1-338-88866-9

Hello, Helpers

By Janice Behrens

Hello, Helpers

By Janice Behrens

No part of this publication can be reproduced in whole or in part, or stored in a retrieval system, or transmitted in any form or by any means, electronic, mechanical, photocopying, recording, or otherwise, without written permission of the publisher. For permission, write to Scholastic Inc., 557 Broadway, New York, NY 10012.

ISBN: 978-1-338-88867-6

Editor: Liza Charlesworth
Art Director: Tannaz Fassihi; Designer: Tanya Chernyak
Photos ©: 2: wavebreakmedia/Shutterstock.com. All other photos © Getty Images.

Copyright © Scholastic Inc. All rights reserved. Published by Scholastic Inc.
1 2 3 4 5 6 7 8 9 10   68   31 30 29 28 27 26 25 24 23
Printed in Jiaxing, China. First printing, January 2023.

SCHOLASTIC INC.

Many people help in our town.
Let's wave to them
as we go around.

There is a crossing guard.
She holds a stop sign.
Hello, helper!

There is a firefighter.
He rides in the truck.
Hello, helper!

There is a mail carrier.
She brings the mail.
Hello, helper!

There is a baker.
He bakes yummy bread.
Hello, helper!

There is a construction worker.
She hammers a nail.
Hello, helper!

There is a teacher.
She helps, too.
She reads a book to me and you!

Let's Find Out
Readers

ISBN: 978-1-338-88867-6

Let's Find Out Readers

Time for a Check Up

By Janice Behrens

Scholastic

Time for a Checkup

By Janice Behrens

No part of this publication can be reproduced in whole or in part, or stored in a retrieval system, or transmitted in any form or by any means, electronic, mechanical, photocopying, recording, or otherwise, without written permission of the publisher. For permission, write to Scholastic Inc., 557 Broadway, New York, NY 10012.

ISBN: 978-1-338-88868-3

Editor: Liza Charlesworth
Art Director: Tannaz Fassihi; Designer: Tanya Chernyak
Photos ©: 7: LightField Studios/Shutterstock.com; 8: Rawpixel.com/Shutterstock.com.
All other photos © Getty Images.

Copyright © Scholastic Inc. All rights reserved. Published by Scholastic Inc.

1 2 3 4 5 6 7 8 9 10   68   31 30 29 28 27 26 25 24 23

Printed in Jiaxing, China. First printing, January 2023.

SCHOLASTIC INC.

How is your heart?
Let's check it and see.
Your heart sounds good to me.

How is your nose?
Let's check it and see.
Your nose looks good to me.

How is your ear?
Let's check it and see.
Your ear looks good to me.

How is your eye?
Let's check it and see.
Your eye looks good to me.

How is your mouth?
Let's check it and see.
Your mouth looks good to me.

How is your foot?
Let's check it and see.
Your foot looks good to me.

How is your bear?
Let's check it and see.
Your bear looks good to me!

ISBN: 978-1-338-88868-3

Let's Find Out Readers

D

City Life, Country Life

By Pamela Chanko

SCHOLASTIC

City Life, Country Life

By Pamela Chanko

No part of this publication can be reproduced in whole or in part, or stored in a retrieval system, or transmitted in any form or by any means, electronic, mechanical, photocopying, recording, or otherwise, without written permission of the publisher. For permission, write to Scholastic Inc., 557 Broadway, New York, NY 10012.

ISBN: 978-1-338-88869-0

Editor: Liza Charlesworth
Art Director: Tannaz Fassihi; Designer: Tanya Chernyak
Photos ©: 5: Hongqi Zhang/Alamy Stock Photo; 7: Tetra Images/Alamy Stock Photo; 8: Tetra Images/Alamy Stock Photo. All other photos © Shutterstock.com.

Copyright © Scholastic Inc. All rights reserved. Published by Scholastic Inc.
1 2 3 4 5 6 7 8 9 10   68   31 30 29 28 27 26 25 24 23
Printed in Jiaxing, China. First printing, January 2023.

SCHOLASTIC INC.

What can you do in the city?
You can see tall buildings.
Let's go there!

What can you do in the country?
You can see big barns.
Let's go there!

What can you do in the city?
You can cross a busy street.
Let's go there!

What can you do in the country?
You can cross a quiet stream.
Let's go there!

What can you do in the city?
You can ride in a yellow taxi.
Let's go there!

What can you do in the country?
You can ride on a green tractor.
Let's go there!

What can you do in both places?
You can make a new friend.
Let's go there!

ISBN: 978-1-338-88869-0

Let's Find Out Readers

At the Fair

By Janice Behrens

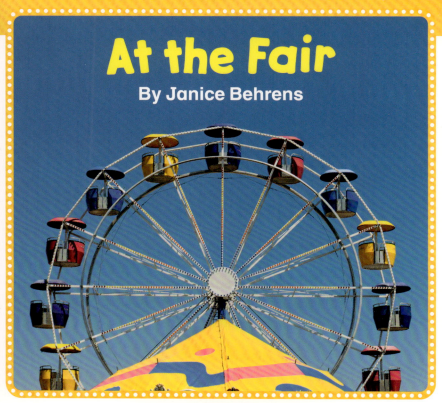

Scholastic

At the Fair

By Janice Behrens

No part of this publication can be reproduced in whole or in part, or stored in a retrieval system, or transmitted in any form or by any means, electronic, mechanical, photocopying, recording, or otherwise, without written permission of the publisher. For permission, write to Scholastic Inc., 557 Broadway, New York, NY 10012.

ISBN: 978-1-338-88870-6

Editor: Liza Charlesworth
Art Director: Tannaz Fassihi; Designer: Tanya Chernyak
Photos ©: cover: Holly Kuchera/Shutterstock.com; 4: Cheryl Casey/Shutterstock.com.
All other photos © Getty Images.

Copyright © Scholastic Inc. All rights reserved. Published by Scholastic Inc.
1 2 3 4 5 6 7 8 9 10   68   31 30 29 28 27 26 25 24 23
Printed in Jiaxing, China. First printing, January 2023.

SCHOLASTIC INC.

Today is the day.
Let's go to the fair.
We can go on a ride there.
Wheeeeee!

Today is the day.
Let's go to the fair.
We can see a sheep there.
Baa!

Today is the day.
Let's go to the fair.
We can eat corn there.
Yum!

Today is the day.
Let's go to the fair.
We can drive a car there.
Vroom!

Today is the day.
Let's go to the fair.
We can play a game there.
Bop!

Today is the day.
Let's go to the fair.
We can jump up and down there.
Boing!

Tonight is the night.
Let's go to the fair.
We can see fireworks there.
Boom! Boom! Wow!

ISBN: 978-1-338-88870-6